Table of Contents

WRITING THE BEST ANNOTATED BIBLIOGRAPHY 1

WWW.CUTEWRITERS.COM 1

In case you wish to learn more about scholarly writing and copywriting, please visit www.cutewriters.com 3

What is a bibliography? 3

What is an annotation? 4

What is an Annotated Bibliography? 5

What are the differences between annotated bibliographies and normal bibliographies? 7

The Main components 10

- **Full bibliographic citation** 10
- **Author's Background** 10
- **Purpose of the work** 10
- **The Scope of the work** 10
- **Main argument** 10
- **Audience** 11
- **Methodology** 11
- **Viewpoint** 11
- **Sources** 11
- **Reliability of the source** 12
- **Conclusion** 12
- **Features** 12
- **Strengths and Weaknesses** 12

- Comparison 12
- Your Voice / Personal Conclusion 13

What is the Purpose of an Annotated Bibliography? 13

    The DON'TS when writing your annotated bibliography 14

    Types of annotated bibliographies 15

Summary annotations 16

    Critical / Evaluative annotations 18

    Combination annotations 19

    Structure of an annotated bibliography 19

How to write an annotated bibliography 20

    Questions that should guide you when setting out to write an annotated bibliography 22

    Summarising the source material 23

    Assessing the source material 24

    Reflecting on the source material 26

    Why should you write an annotated bibliography? 27

        What are the differences between an annotated bibliography and an abstract? 30

        How to do Critical Appraisal of Books, Articles, Or Documents 32

Choosing the best formatting style... 32

    How to choose the appropriate style / format for the citations of your annotated bibliography 32

    Formats of writing annotated bibliographies 33

        The bibliographic information 34

        The annotations 35

Examples of Annotated Bibliography Entry for A Journal Article 36

   APA format annotated bibliography: 36

   MLA format annotated bibliography 37

See the most frequently asked questions by our visitors and clients 39

References and Further Reading 43

WRITING THE BEST ANNOTATED BIBLIOGRAPHY

WWW.CUTEWRITERS.COM

About The Author

Kegesa Danvas Abdullah is the founder of Cute Writers, a Copywriting Company and the Cute Online Money Empire.

He wants you to grasp the art and science of writing scholarly papers excellently

In case of any comments, questions, concerns, or corrections please contact me:

Danvas@CuteOnlineMoney.com

You can also connect with me on:

My Blog

Facebook

Google Plus

Twitter

In case you wish to learn more about scholarly writing and copywriting, please visit www.cutewriters.com

What is a bibliography?

Before you understand what an annotated bibliography is, you should know what the term "bibliography" means.

A Bibliography is a list of sources (books, journals, Web sites, periodicals, articles, newspapers, sections of books, etc.) that one has employed in their research.

Bibliographies are sometimes called "References" or "Works Cited" depending on the citation, referencing style or format you are using. A bibliography usually just includes the bibliographic information (i.e., the author, title, publisher, etc.).

What is an annotation?

An **annotation** is a summary and/or descriptive and analytical evaluation of the source. An annotation briefly reiterates the main argument of a source.

An annotation of an academic source, for example, typically identifies its thesis (or research question, or hypothesis), its primary methods of investigation, and its key findings.

Keep in mind that identifying the argument of a source is a different task than describing or listing its contents.

Rather than listing contents, an annotation further accounts for the inclusion of the materials that are in the source.

What is an Annotated Bibliography?

The synonym word for annotated is "explained, interpreted, marked up, noted, marked or glossed". This implies that an annotated bibliography is a described regular bibliography that is written at the end of a written document.

The explanation and interpretation form the comments which are also referred to as annotations.

The standard definition of an annotated bibliography "is a list of citations to books, articles, and documents which contain a brief descriptive or evaluative paragraph of the work included in the sources."
In other words, an *annotated bibliography* or annotated bib is a bibliography (a list of books or other works) that includes descriptive and evaluative comments on the sources cited in your paper.

An annotated bibliography provides a brief account of the available research on a given topic. It is a list of research sources that includes succinct descriptions and evaluations of each source. The annotation also contains a brief summary of content and a short analysis or evaluation. Depending on your assignment you may be asked to reflect, summarize, critique, evaluate or analyze the source.

What are the differences between annotated bibliographies and normal bibliographies?

The main difference between annotated bibliographies and the standard straightforward bibliographies is that each reference in the annotated bibliography is followed by a paragraph length annotation, usually 100–200 words in length, unlike in ordinary lists at the end of written documents.

Like any bibliography, the entries or research sources in an annotated bibliography are alphabetically listed.

In addition to bibliographic data; an annotated bibliography provides a concise summary of each source and some assessment of its value or relevance.

Depending on your assignment, an annotated bibliography may be one stage of a larger research project, or it may be an independent project standing on its own.

An annotated bibliography may be a component of a larger project, or it may be a stand-alone assignment.

While an annotation can be as brief as one sentence, the standard annotated bibliography consists of a citation followed by a short paragraph of approximately 150 to 300 words depending on the instructions and the content being interpreted. Therefore, an annotated bibliography includes a summary and some appraisal of each of the sources.

This guide just provides a general guideline using standard procedures; you may seek further clarification from your faculty members for specific instructions.

The Main components

- **Full bibliographic citation**

  An annotated bibliography must contain the necessary and **complete bibliographical information i.e.** (author, title, publisher and date, etc.),

- **Author's Background**

  You should provide the name, authority, experience, or qualifications of the author.

- **Purpose of the work**

  You should provide the reasons why the author wrote the work

- **The Scope of the work**

  You should state the breadth or depth of coverage and topics or sub-topics covered.

- **Main argument**

State the main informative points of the paper

- **Audience**

  For whom was it written (general public, subject specialists, students…)?

- **Methodology**

  What methodology and research methods did the work employ?

- **Viewpoint**

  What is the author's perspective or approach (school of thought, etc.)? Do you detect an unacknowledged bias, or find any undefended assumptions?

- **Sources**

  Does the author cite other sources, and if so, what types? Is it based on the author's own research? Is it personal opinion? …

- **Reliability of the source**

    How reliable is the work?

- **Conclusion**

- What does the author conclude about the work? Is the conclusion justified by the work?

- **Features**

    Any significant extras, e.g. visual aids (charts, maps, etc.), reprints of source documents, an annotated bibliography?

- **Strengths and Weaknesses**

    What are the strengths and weaknesses of the work?

- **Comparison**

    How does the source relate to other works done by other writers on the topic: does it agree or disagree with another author or a particular school of thought; are there other works which would support or dispute it?

- **Your Voice / Personal Conclusion**

    Provide your point of view of the work or your reaction to the source based on other available works, prior knowledge of the subject matter or knowledge pools done by other researchers.

What is the Purpose of an Annotated Bibliography?

This answers the question "Why are annotated bibliographies so important for the students or researchers?"

The annotated bibliography serves many purposes including the following; informing the reader of the summary, relevance, accuracy, and quality of the sources cited.

The DON'TS when writing your annotated bibliography

In-text Citations: Since annotations are written below the bibliography referenced, it is not necessary to write in-text citations. The in-text citations are only used in the main document.

Writing Too Much: Annotations should be concise and to the point. Save your many words for the thesis, book, dissertation or research paper.

Writing a summary: Annotations are not mere summaries. Unless stated otherwise, you must have assessments and evaluations of the most important points after which you weigh the strengths and weaknesses and then present your perspective. You shall find more on this as you read this document.

Types of annotated bibliographies

It is impossible to describe a standard procedure for all kinds of annotations because one annotation does not fit all purposes.

There are diverse types of annotations, depending on what might be most important for your reader or according to your professor's instructions.

To know the best type of annotated bibliography, it is prudent to consult your instructor or follow the instructions.

For example, if the assignment states that your annotative bibliography should give evidence proving an analytical understanding of the sources you have used, then you are supposed to write an analytical annotated bibliography which includes evaluation of the sources you are using.

There are three types of annotated bibliographies; summary annotations, critical annotations and a combination of both.

Summary annotations

Summary annotations are further classified into informative and indicative annotations.

The following are the main features of summary annotations:

- They show an account of the source content
- They highlight the arguments and proofs/evidence mentioned in the work

- They sometimes describe the author's methodology and any theories used
- They offer the conclusion of the source
- They do not evaluate the work they are discussing

Informative annotated bibliographies

Informative annotations provide a straight summary of the origin material. They summarize all relevant information about the author and the main points of the work. To write it, begin by writing the thesis; then develop it with the argument or hypothesis, list the proofs, and state the conclusion.

Indicative annotated bibliographies

Indicative annotations do not provide actual information from the source.

They provide overall information about what kinds of questions or issues are addressed by the work, for example, through chapter titles.

In the indicative entry, there is no attempt to give actual data such as hypotheses, proofs, etc.

Critical / Evaluative annotations

This is the second classification of annotated bibliographies.

Evaluative annotated bibliographies do more than just summarizing; they provide critical appraisals. It evaluates the source or author critically to find any biases, lack of evidence, objectives, etc.

It shows how the work may or may not be useful for a particular field of study or audience.

It explains how researching this material assisted your own project.

Combination annotations

This type of annotated bibliography combines elements of all the types listed above. Many annotations fall into this category: They are made from a little summarizing and describing, a little evaluation of the sources.

Structure of an annotated bibliography

Length: Annotations should be one paragraph long. Many annotations are written in approximately 100 to 200 words with a goal of brief and explicative annotations

Person: The third person is the regular person of expression though the first person may be appropriate for certain types of annotated bibliographies and for presenting your personal opinions.

Language and Vocabulary: Annotations use official language. It is important to use the author's vocabulary correctly to convey the ideas and conclusions of the author without losing meaning. In all cases, avoid vague statements.

Sentence Format: Always use whole sentences. Single and straightforward descriptive words and phrases or lists may also be used.

How to write an annotated bibliography

The process of writing annotated bibliographies is easy.

In this section, you shall learn how to make your annotated bibliography step by step.

Writing an annotated bibliography depends on the type of work for which you are writing, the writing style used and university regulations.

In all cases, please follow the instructions given by your instructors if in doubt of anything.

It is important to adhere to the professor's directions because word length, citation styles and some formatting styles vary from one learning institution to another.

Creating an annotated bibliography calls for the application of a variety of intellectual skills:

concise exposition, succinct analysis, and informed library research.

First, locate and record citations to books, periodicals, and documents that may contain useful information and ideas on your topic. Briefly, examine and review the actual items.

Then choose those works that provide a variety of perspectives on your topic.

The specified length of your explanations will determine how detailed your summary is.

Questions that should guide you when setting out to write an annotated bibliography

1. What topic/ problem are you investigating?

2. What question(s) are you exploring?

3. What is the aim of your literature research?

4. What kinds of material are you looking at and why?

5. Are you looking for journal articles, reports, policies or primary historical data?

6. Are you judicious in your selection of texts?

7. Does each text relate to your research topic and assignment requirements?

8. What are the essential or critical texts on your topic?

9. Are you finding the important points relevant to the current study?

10. Are the sources valuable or often referred to in other texts?

Summarising the source material

The annotated bibliography should provide a brief summary of the source.

An annotated bibliography gives an account of the research that has been done on a given topic. To write the best summary, you should ask yourself the following questions:

1. Who is the author of the source material?
2. What are the author's main arguments in the source?
3. What is the point of this book or article?
4. What topics are covered?
5. If you are asked for the general information in the source, what would you say?

Assessing the source material

After creating a summary of the source, it is prudent and helpful to evaluate it. Ask yourself some of the following questions:

1. Was the source useful?
2. Does this article fill a gap in literature?
3. How would you be able to apply this method/study to your particular study?
4. Is the article universal?
5. Did it provide the necessary information about the topic you were researching?
6. What information is missing according to other authors?
7. How does the information in the source compare with other sources in your bibliography?

8. Can you rely on the information provided by the source?
9. Does the author of the source have any biasedness or objective?
10. What is the goal of the source?
11. What is the tone of the author?

Reflecting on the source material

After summarizing and assessing the annotated bibliography, it is important to ask how it fits into your research.

Some of the questions answered in this section of the annotated bibliography include the following:

1. Was the source helpful to you?
2. How does the source help in shaping your argument?

3. How can the source assist you in carrying out your research project successfully?
4. Has the source changed how you think about your topic?

Why should you write an annotated bibliography?

Writing an annotated bibliography is the best preparation for writing a research project. In as much as collecting sources for a bibliography is useful; writing annotations for all sources enhances better understanding of the sources. Writing an annotated bibliography enables you to read more critically instead of just collecting information.

Professional authors and researchers use annotated bibliographies at professional levels to determine the research topics which have already been done in their areas of study. Therefore, the annotated bibliography helps in identifying research gaps which should be bridged.

The annotated bibliographies help researchers and writers to formulate a good thesis through the arguments generated and support it through the evidence gathered. Since the development of a debatable, interesting, and current thesis is a crucial stage in writing dissertations, theses and research papers, annotations are necessary. Annotations help you in finding what other researchers have said about the research topic and the most current information about a particular subject.

By reading and reacting to a variety of sources on a particular topic, you will start seeing what the issues are, what people are arguing about, and you will then be able to develop your point of view.

Annotations help you in presenting your own point of view on a given topic. It allows you to agree, disagree or critique the source.

Your extensive and scholarly annotated bibliography may help other researchers in your field especially if it is published.

By writing the annotated bibliography, you will learn more about your topic, become an expert and understand the topic better

It helps in reviewing works of other people and enhances your research and writing skills.

The annotated bibliography helps to display the depth and quality of the reading that you have done. When set as an assignment, an annotated bibliography allows you to get acquainted with the material available on a particular topic.

The annotations provide insights on the available sources such as books, journals, articles, magazines and websites that contain useful information that may be of interest to other readers and researchers

What are the differences between an annotated bibliography and an abstract?

Annotated bibliographies are descriptive and critical; they explain more about the author's point of view, clarity and appropriateness of expression, and authority in addition to giving a brief summary.

Annotated bibliographies are standalone in that; no full document comes after the annotations.

Annotations are typically written by a different person other than the author of the work.

Abstracts are the purely descriptive summaries often found at the beginning of scholarly journal articles or in periodical indexes.

Abstracts do not have any critical appraisal or the author's perspective of the work.

Abstracts are written to capture the summary of a written work, usually at the beginning of the work, to give a general overview. Abstracts are written by the author of the work.

How to do Critical Appraisal of Books, Articles, Or Documents

If you want to do the key assessment of any written document, you should click this link on guidance in critically appraising and analyzing the sources for your bibliography, How to Critically Analyze Information Sources.

Choosing the best formatting style

How to choose the appropriate style / format for the citations of your annotated bibliography

Annotated bibliographies are written according to standard citation styles.

The most common citation/ referencing styles include Modern Language Association (MLA) and the American Psychological Association (APA) styles, Harvard, Chicago, Turabian, ISO 690, GHOST, IEEE, Oxford, AMA, ASA, Vancouver and many others.

Before you can use any style, please consult your instructor to find out which style is preferred for your class.

You may also check the assignment specifications or in your university or college website.

Formats of writing annotated bibliographies

Annotated bibliographies contain two main sections; the bibliographic information section and the annotations section.

Since the formats may slightly vary from one institution to another depending on the regulations, courses and materials being annotated, it is imperative to ask for specific guidelines.

The bibliographic information

The bibliographic information is written before the annotation using the suitable referencing style. The information is typically indented using a hanging indent.

Though, the bibliographic information of the source (the title, author, publisher, date, etc.) is written in either MLA or APA format. For more help with formatting, you can learn more here MLA handout for MLA or visit APA handout for APA.

The annotations

The annotations for each source are written in paragraph form. The lengths of the annotations can vary significantly from a couple of sentences to a couple of pages. The length will depend on the purpose. If you're just writing summaries of your sources, the annotations may not be very long. However, if you are writing an extensive analysis of each source, you'll need more space. You can focus your annotations for your needs. A few sentences of general summary followed by several sentences of how you can fit the work into your larger paper or project can serve you well when you go to the draft.

Examples of Annotated Bibliography Entry for A Journal Article

APA format annotated bibliography:

Waite, L. J., Goldschneider, F. K., & Witsberger, C. (1986). Nonfamily living and the erosion of traditional family orientations among young adults. *American Sociological Review,* **51 (4), 541-554.**

The authors, researchers at the Rand Corporation and Brown University, use data from the National Longitudinal Surveys of Young Women and Young Men to test their hypothesis that nonfamily living by young adults alters their attitudes, values, plans, and expectations, moving them away from their belief in traditional sex roles. They find their hypothesis strongly supported in young females, while the effects were fewer in studies of young males. Increasing the time away from parents before marrying increased individualism, self-sufficiency, and changes in attitudes about families. In contrast, an earlier study by Williams cited below shows no significant gender differences in sex role attitudes as a result of nonfamily living.

MLA format annotated bibliography

Note that the MLA style employs double spacing within citations.

Waite, Linda J., Frances Kobrin Goldscheider, and Christina Witsberger. "Nonfamily Living and the Erosion of Traditional Family

Orientations Among Young Adults." *American Sociological Review* 51.4 (1986): 541-554. Print.

The authors, researchers at the Rand Corporation and Brown University, use data from the National Longitudinal Surveys of Young Women and Young Men to test their hypothesis that nonfamily living by young adults alters their attitudes, values, plans, and expectations, moving them away from their belief in traditional sex roles. They find their hypothesis strongly supported in young females, while the effects were fewer in studies of young males. Increasing the time away from parents before marrying increased individualism, self-sufficiency, and changes in attitudes about families. In contrast, an earlier study by Williams cited below shows no significant gender differences in sex role attitudes as a result of nonfamily living.

See the most frequently asked questions by our visitors and clients

What is an annotated bibliography?

Can someone write my annotated bibliography?

Who can help make an annotated bibliography essay?

How much time does it take to write an annotation?

Is it easy to write an annotated bibliography?

What is the best annotated Bibliography writing service?

What skills are necessary to write an excellent annotated bibliography?

Do I have to read the whole source material to write an annotated bibliography?

Can I purchase an annotated bibliography online?

What is the best annotation writing company in the world?

What if my teacher gives me instructions which are different from the guidelines provided on your website?

Is it legal to buy writing services or to outsource writers?

Are APA, MLA or Harvard Annotated Bibliography annotated bibliographies similar?

What are the differences among high school, college, university or PhD annotated bibliographies?

I want someone to write my annotated bibliography for me free

Write my annotated bibliography for me now

Who will write my annotated bibliography for me now?

What are the leading companies that write annotated bibliography online?

Can you help me write an annotated bibliography rubric for my class?

What is the best format for custom annotated bibliography writing?

Can I get a well-organized custom annotated bibliography from your writing company?

Are annotated bibliographies double spaced or single spaced?

Can you tell me Best Places to Buy American English Annotated Bibliography Online 24/7?

Will you guys send APA, MLA, Harvard, and Chicago, AMA or ASA examples or templates of annotated bibliographies to me if I give you my email?

Are there easier and cheaper ways of writing annotated bibliographies?

Is it good to use an online bibliography makers or online bibliography and reference creator websites?

Can you suggest possible research topics and send them to me as doc, pdf or docx so that I write an annotation?

Am I supposed to write my annotated bibliography citations in alphabetical order in my assignment sheet?

What should I write on the cover page of my annotated bibliography?

Should the APA and MLA annotated bibliography be double spaced or single spaced?

Are there any checkers for annotated bibliographies?

What are the best essay topics for which I can write an annotated bibliography for college admission?

References and Further Reading

For further studies on annotated bibliographies, please refer to the following references:

Annotated Bibliography." The Writing Center. 2003. University of Wisconsin, Madison. 5 March 2004 <http://www.wisc.edu/writing/Handbook/AnnotatedBibliography.html>.

Concordia University Library Annotated Bibliography Guide

The University of California, Santa Cruz Annotated Bibliography Guide

Cutewriters Custom Writing Service

There are many resources in the internet about annotated bibliography sources, annotation databases, sample annotated bibliography papers, annotated bibliography examples, annotated bibliography articles, guidelines on how to write an annotated bibliography paper, how to do annotated bibliography dissertation, how to prepare a good annotated bibliography, writing the definition introduction and literature review-based annotations and many more.

With many resources in the internet, it is not easy to determine the best annotated bibliography sites, services and resources which can help scholars to write the highest quality and original annotated bibliography papers.

It is our belief that this guide becomes your best annotated bibliography guide to help you write professional annotated bibliographies.

If you are unable to write a high-quality annotated bibliography after reading this document, please contact us for a free template and for premium help.

We already know the importance of an annotated bibliography in your research paper.

Our company has many experienced and professional writers who are devoted in helping our visitors and clients in writing all types of bibliographies.

Our expert writers are knowledgeable in writing all types of annotated bibliographies in all formats.

Cutewriters delivers annotated bibliographies of research papers, journals, theses, dissertations, books, articles and all types of written work. It is easy to get help writing your annotated bibliography in all styles including MLA annotated bibliography, APA annotated bibliography, and Harvard style annotated bibliography, Chicago style of annotated bibliography, Turabian style. This annotated bibliography guide also has annotated bibliography examples to help you in formulating the best custom bibliography. We have provided APA and MLA annotated bibliography templates in this annotation template. In case you need other formats, feel free to contact us through the details in the contact us page. We are among the leading companies or services which provide free and premium annotated bibliography writing services.

If you order your paper, we shall provide a nice free annotated bibliography along with the paper. We only offer tutoring services for standalone annotations.

In case you need expert help in writing your annotated bibliography, please visit Cutewriters.com and Order the Services

<u>Order Best Annotated Bibliography Writing Service</u>

Made in the USA
Columbia, SC
06 October 2020